Creepy Creatures

SHOEBILLS

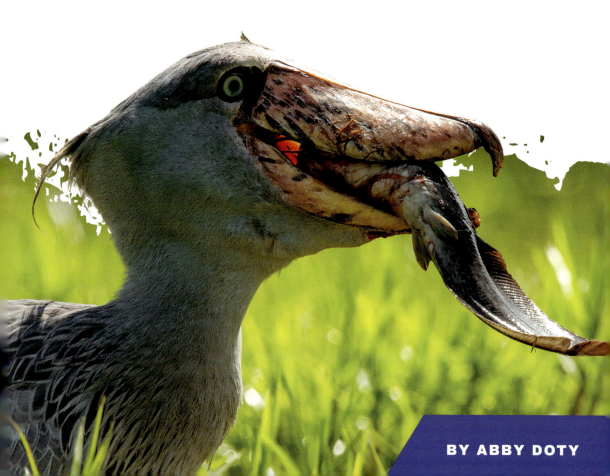

BY ABBY DOTY

WWW.APEXEDITIONS.COM

Copyright © 2025 by Apex Editions, Mendota Heights, MN 55120. All rights reserved. No part of this book may be reproduced or utilized in any form or by any means without written permission from the publisher.

Apex is distributed by North Star Editions:
sales@northstareditions.com | 888-417-0195

Produced for Apex by Red Line Editorial.

Photographs ©: Shutterstock Images, cover, 1, 4–5, 6–7, 8–9, 14, 15, 16–17, 18–19, 20–21, 24, 26–27; iStockphoto, 10–11, 12–13, 22–23, 29; Barrie Britton/Nature Picture Library/Alamy, 25

Library of Congress Control Number: 2024944013

ISBN
979-8-89250-322-8 (hardcover)
979-8-89250-360-0 (paperback)
979-8-89250-434-8 (ebook pdf)
979-8-89250-398-3 (hosted ebook)

Printed in the United States of America
Mankato, MN
012025

NOTE TO PARENTS AND EDUCATORS

Apex books are designed to build literacy skills in striving readers. Exciting, high-interest content attracts and holds readers' attention. The text is carefully leveled to allow students to achieve success quickly. Additional features, such as bolded glossary words for difficult terms, help build comprehension.

TABLE OF CONTENTS

CHAPTER 1
SNEAK ATTACK 4

CHAPTER 2
BIG BEAKS 10

CHAPTER 3
LIFE IN THE WILD 16

CHAPTER 4
LIFE CYCLE 22

COMPREHENSION QUESTIONS • 28
GLOSSARY • 30
TO LEARN MORE • 31
ABOUT THE AUTHOR • 31
INDEX • 32

CHAPTER 1

SNEAK ATTACK

A shoebill stands completely still in a **marsh**. A few fish swim by. The shoebill's eyes lock onto one. Suddenly, the bird attacks.

Shoebills may stand still for hours before striking.

The shoebill drops to the water. Its beak snaps shut. The fish tries to squirm away. But the shoebill holds tight and gulps it down.

FAST FACT

Shoebills often hunt large **prey**, such as lungfish. Some even eat baby crocodiles.

After catching a fish, a shoebill often swings its head from side to side to get rid of plants and mud.

When flying, shoebills flap their wings about 150 times per minute.

Ready for more food, the shoebill flaps its wings. It flies to another part of the marsh. There, the bird holds still again. It waits for its next meal.

COOLING OFF

Shoebills often stand under the sun while hunting. Sometimes, they need to cool off. So, they pee on their legs. The pee works like sweat. It cools the birds when it **evaporates**.

CHAPTER 2

Big Beaks

Shoebills can grow to be 5 feet (1.5 m) tall. But they only weigh up to 12 pounds (5.4 kg). The birds have gray and white feathers.

Shoebills can have yellow, green, or blue eyes. The birds rarely blink.

Shoebills have huge beaks. Some are 12 inches (30 cm) long. The birds use their beaks to make clapping noises. These sounds can scare off animals or help a shoebill find a **mate**.

FAST FACT

The shoebill has the third-longest beak of any bird.

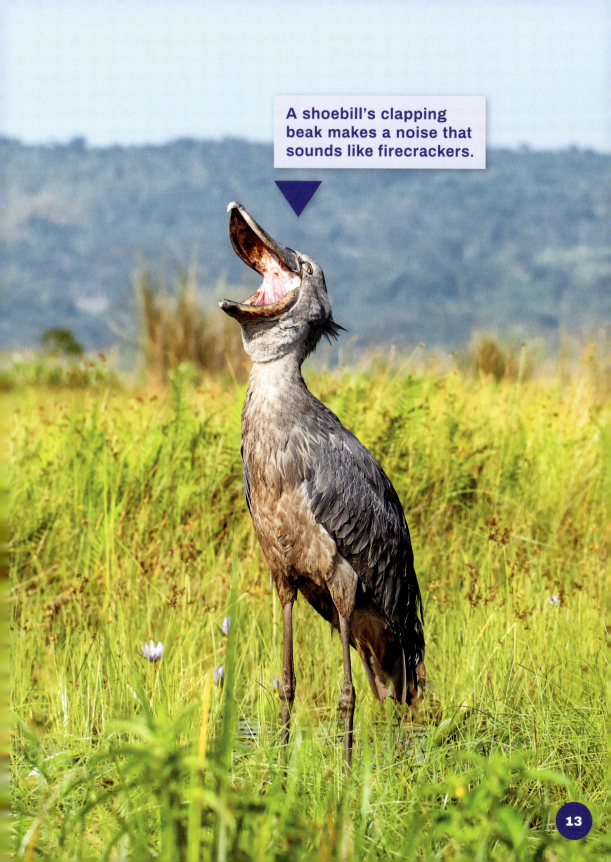

A shoebill's clapping beak makes a noise that sounds like firecrackers.

Shoebills hunt in **shallow** water. They stay still until prey comes close. Then, the birds strike quickly. They often eat fish, lizards, and snakes.

Shoebills can go four days without eating.

Shoebills usually bite the head off their prey before swallowing.

SUPER SHARP

A shoebill's beak ends in a hook. The hook can stab prey. It helps the bird hold on to slippery food. The beak also has sharp edges. Those help cut prey apart.

CHAPTER 3

LIFE IN THE WILD

Shoebills live in eastern and central Africa. The birds can be found in freshwater **swamps** and marshes that have lots of plants.

Shoebills stay hidden among tall reeds and grasses.

FAST FACT
Shoebills can fly up to 30 miles per hour (48 km/h).

Shoebills have long legs and toes. They have strong wings, too. These body parts help shoebills balance while walking through wet and muddy areas.

Shoebills have wingspans of about 8 feet (2.4 m).

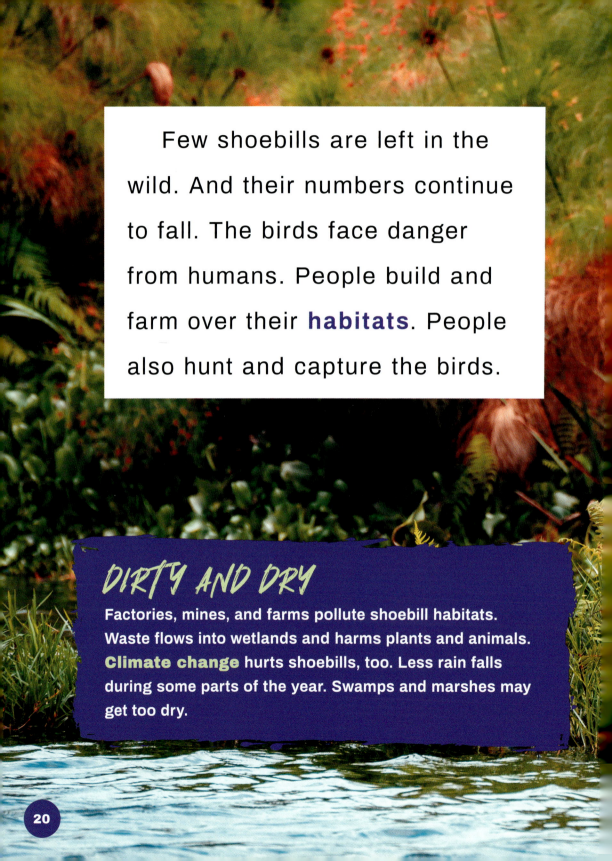

Few shoebills are left in the wild. And their numbers continue to fall. The birds face danger from humans. People build and farm over their **habitats**. People also hunt and capture the birds.

DIRTY AND DRY

Factories, mines, and farms pollute shoebill habitats. Waste flows into wetlands and harms plants and animals. **Climate change** hurts shoebills, too. Less rain falls during some parts of the year. Swamps and marshes may get too dry.

Scientists think there are between 3,300 and 5,300 adult shoebills left in the wild.

CHAPTER 4

LIFE CYCLE

Shoebills live alone. But they come together to find mates. The parents build nests among tall plants. Some nests float on top of the water. Others are built on islands.

Shoebills make their nests out of grasses and other plants.

Both shoebill parents care for eggs. They often spit water onto the eggs to keep them cool.

Shoebills usually lay two eggs at a time. For 30 days, parents take turns sitting on their eggs. Once the eggs hatch, the parents bring food to the chicks.

ONLY ONE

Usually, only one shoebill chick survives. Some babies are killed by **predators**. Other times, chicks fight each other. Parents only feed and care for the strongest baby.

Shoebill chicks may kill each other in fights.

Chicks start with soft, fluffy feathers. About three months after hatching, they finish growing feathers for flying. A month after that, young shoebills can live on their own.

FAST FACT
Shoebills can live for up to 35 years in the wild.

◀ Shoebills can have their own chicks after three to four years.

COMPREHENSION QUESTIONS

Write your answers on a separate piece of paper.

1. Write a few sentences explaining the main ideas of Chapter 2.

2. Which fact about shoebills do you think is creepiest? Why?

3. How much do shoebills weigh?
   - A. up to 5 pounds (2.3 kg)
   - B. up to 12 pounds (5.4 kg)
   - C. up to 30 pounds (14 kg)

4. At what age can young shoebills live on their own?
   - A. one month
   - B. three months
   - C. four months

5. What does **pollute** mean in this book?

*Factories, mines, and farms **pollute** shoebill habitats. Waste flows into wetlands and harms plants and animals.*

- **A.** to make dirty or unsafe
- **B.** to help and heal
- **C.** to stay away from

6. What does **survives** mean in this book?

*Usually, only one shoebill chick **survives**. Some babies are killed by predators.*

- **A.** comes from an egg
- **B.** stays alive
- **C.** dies

Answer key on page 32.

GLOSSARY

climate change
A dangerous long-term change in Earth's temperature and weather patterns.

evaporates
Changes from a liquid to a gas.

habitats
The places where animals normally live.

marsh
A grassy wetland that is similar to a swamp.

mate
One of a pair of animals that come together to have babies.

predators
Animals that hunt and eat other animals.

prey
Animals that are hunted and eaten by other animals.

shallow
Not deep.

swamps
Areas of low land covered in water, often with many plants.

TO LEARN MORE

BOOKS

Hansen, Grace. *Shoebills*. Minneapolis: Abdo Publishing, 2021.

Johnson, Robin. *Shoebill*. New York: Crabtree Publishing, 2024.

Wilson, Libby. *Bizarre Birds*. Mendota Heights, MN: Apex Editions, 2024.

ONLINE RESOURCES

Visit **www.apexeditions.com** to find links and resources related to this title.

ABOUT THE AUTHOR

Abby Doty is a writer, editor, and booklover from Minnesota.

INDEX

A
Africa, 16

B
beaks, 6, 12, 15

C
chicks, 24–25, 27
climate change, 20

E
eggs, 24

F
feathers, 10, 27

H
habitats, 20
hook, 15
humans, 20

M
marshes, 4, 9, 16, 20
mates, 12, 22

N
nests, 22

P
predators, 25
prey, 6, 14–15

S
swamps, 16, 20

W
wings, 9, 18

ANSWER KEY:
1. Answers will vary; 2. Answers will vary; 3. B; 4. C; 5. A; 6. B